John S. Billings, Henry M. Hurd, Silas W. Mitchell

**Suggestions to Hospital and Asylum Visitors**

John S. Billings, Henry M. Hurd, Silas W. Mitchell

**Suggestions to Hospital and Asylum Visitors**

ISBN/EAN: 9783337161828

Printed in Europe, USA, Canada, Australia, Japan

Cover: Foto ©Andreas Hilbeck / pixelio.de

More available books at **www.hansebooks.com**

# SUGGESTIONS

TO

# HOSPITAL AND ASYLUM

# VISITORS.

BY

## JOHN S. BILLINGS, M.D.,

DIRECTOR OF THE HOSPITAL OF THE UNIVERSITY OF PENNSYLVANIA,

AND

## HENRY M. HURD, M.D.,

SUPERINTENDENT OF THE JOHNS HOPKINS HOSPITAL.

WITH AN INTRODUCTION
BY S. WEIR MITCHELL, M.D.

---

PHILADELPHIA:

J. B. LIPPINCOTT COMPANY.

1895.

# INTRODUCTION.

FOR several years I have been urging upon Professor Billings the need for a small manual suited to the wants of hospital visitors. I have many times been asked by laymen who have to manage eleemosynary institutions where they could learn how critically to inspect them with a reasonable chance of seeing what is wrong and learning how to value what is praiseworthy. It is useless to point the inquirer to the greater works on hygiene. These presuppose such knowledge as few possess who are not educated physicians. There is needed a condensed statement of *what* to see in a hospital and *how* to see it.

Every new domain of observation requires a peculiar and individualized training. The acute microscopist might be a dull observer of the facts of disease which we call symptoms; the clever artist may be a sad failure when called upon to see with critical eyes the phenomena of the laboratory. How, then, can we expect that quite untrained people should of a sudden become useful observers in a field as new to them as is a hospital.

Boards of managers are chosen out of the every-day life of commerce and professions other than that of medicine. The members are presumed to study results into which enter questions of cooking, dietetics, ventilation, medical and surgical cleanliness, which involves disinfection, and many other matters exacting careful attention, and only to be thoroughly understood after years of training. This little manual is meant to assist untrained observers, yet even the most expert manager of a hospital or the ablest medical observer ought to find in it valuable hints.

This guide to the hospital visitor I have asked leave to introduce. It has cost an amount of care and thought out of proportion to its size. While in manuscript it was critically read by Professors J. M. Da Costa, J. William White, and myself, and certain changes or additions were suggested. Finally, Dr. Hurd, the accomplished director of the Johns Hopkins Hospital, was kind enough to associate himself with Professor Billings and to take the utmost interest in the work. Out of their joint labor and the criticism of able physicians and nurses has come at last the helpful little book which originated in my suggestion, and which I confidently commend to all who, being managers, trustees, or in any way connected with hospital work, are not contented to assume an official name and remain ignorant of how honestly to fulfil the duties which should go with it.

S. WEIR MITCHELL, M.D.

# SUGGESTIONS

## TO

# HOSPITAL AND ASYLUM VISITORS.

---

### I.—HOSPITALS.

THE duties of an hospital visitor, and the precise things which he or she is to observe and comment upon, differ in some respects for each hospital or asylum, according to its objects, its plan, its mode of government, its finances, etc.

The following suggestions are not intended for experienced hospital managers, but for men and women who are beginning to take an interest in some particular hospital, and who have little or no knowledge of the details of hospital management,—persons who

9

have been placed on a committee for visiting the institution, and who would like to know what they should do as members of such a committee, what they are expected to look for, or at, in the hospital, how they should make their reports, etc.

A visitor should go to a hospital in a friendly spirit. An intention to criticise the institution because of a preconceived idea that something is wrong should not be entertained. Conceptions of hospital management should not be formed from gossip, the complaints of dissatisfied patients, or the tales of employés who have a grievance. The visitor owes it to any hospital to visit it at first with an impartial mind, and to see and judge of its work for himself.

The first object of such a visitor should be to become acquainted with those charged with the immediate administration of the institution, and, under their guidance, with the rules of the hospital and the methods actually used in admitting, caring for, and disposing of patients, and in obtaining and caring for the supplies. He should feel sure that he understands these things, and that he can look at them from the point of view of the manager and of other officials of the hospital before he attempts to teach or criticise. From the very beginning, if he has good ordinary powers of observation, he will see things which he will think might be improved, but he had better assume at first that there is some reason for the thing which he does not understand, and try to find out what that reason is.

The second object of the hospital visitor is to help the superintendent or manager and the heads of departments, which is to be done by learning what the special difficulties and troubles are which these officers find most difficult to deal with, by encouragement and approval of efforts to maintain cleanliness, good order, and a friendly, home-like spirit throughout the hospital, and by asking questions about doubtful points in order to call attention to matters which may have been unknown to, or overlooked by, the head of a department, without, at first at least, having any appearance of desiring to find fault.

The third object of the hospital visitor should be to ascertain whether the objects of the hospital are being attained, and, if so, whether this is being done at a reasonable cost.

The chief object of an hospital is the care of the sick, but it is very seldom indeed that this is, or should be, its only object.

Every hospital should contribute something to the increase and diffusion of knowledge for the benefit of other sick persons besides those treated in its wards; and it should also be a means of educating and stimulating the people who contribute to its support, not in medical matters, but in a knowledge of the wants of their less fortunate fellow-men, and of the pleasure derivable from helping others. No hospital, however wealthy it may be, has means sufficient to furnish the best known means of treatment and the best care to all who apply to it for relief; and, therefore, either the more costly methods must be omitted or greatly restricted, or a certain number of applicants must be rejected, or, as is usually the case, both these modes of reducing the expense must be resorted to in order to avoid indebtedness.

There are very few, if any, hospitals in which some of the medical staff do not want instruments, apparatus, drugs, or special diets which are not furnished for lack of funds; there is no hospital in which the great majority of the inmates, both employés and patients, do not desire a more varied and costly supply of food than they receive, and there is no hospital in which at times there are not demands for a greater amount of service than the employés can furnish, or than the managers think it proper to pay for.

Each hospital has its own standards on these different points, and the hospital visitor must find out what that standard is—whether it is a reasonable and proper one—and whether it is being lived up to.

A fourth object of the hospital visitor is to keep the board of trustees, or of managers, informed as to the condition of the institution and its needs, as seen from their point of view, and much depends upon the way in which this duty is performed. Nothing is easier than to discover defects in an hospital, especially in one having an hundred beds and upwards, or in one which receives private patients. A little dirt or fluff can usually be seen somewhere; it will be too warm or too cold in some room or corner; the food will not be served to every patient at just the right time or in the best manner; there will be a few articles of soiled bedding or clothing not removed promptly to the laundry; some employé will have given not altogether satisfactory service; in short, if flaws are looked for they can always be found. Many of these things are merely occasional, but inevitable, precisely as they are in the home of the visitor, and the first thing that the visitor should consider in regard to such flaws or complaints is, is this an accidental, temporary thing, or is it a permanent neglect? and this question cannot be answered with certainty by the person who has had no experience in the ways of hospital life.

As a rule, when a visitor discovers something which is, or seems, not satisfactory, the first thing to be done is to call the attention of the person who is supposed to be immediately responsible for the omission or error, and if this is done in the right way, in most cases nothing more is necessary. In military, in railroad, and in business administration

there is what is known as "the regular chan-
nel" for complaints, and it is useful to pre-
serve such a routine in hospital work.

For example, if the visitor thinks that
some part of the hospital is not as clean as
it should be, or hears complaints from some
patient about the food, the attention of the
superintendent should be called to the matter; but if it is a first complaint, it will
usually not be desirable to make a formal
record of it, or to call the attention of the
board of managers to it. Investigate the
matter again at the next visit, and if the
evil has been corrected enough has been
done. If it has not been corrected, then
the report to higher authority may be made.
A superintendent or a physician has good
reason to complain if the first notice that
something wrong has been observed by a
hospital visitor comes, not from the visitor,
but from some other person or persons to
whom the visitor has mentioned the fact.

Complaints made by patients or their friends are not to be ignored; but they should be carefully considered before deciding that they are reasonable and just. Exceptions to the general rules of the hospital are sometimes desirable and proper, but in recommending such exception the danger of the precedent should be borne in mind, and grounds for the charge of favoritism should be carefully avoided. The written or printed rules and regulations for the guidance of employés and patients in an hospital are usually comparatively simple; but in addition to these there are certain customs, methods, and orderly ways of doing things in every hospital which are not reduced to an express code of directions, but with which the visitor should become familiar.

The spirit in which the hospital is conducted should be carefully observed. It should be noted whether medical rounds are made perfunctorily with an evident desire to get through with them as speedily as possible, or whether a keen interest in the excellence of their professional work is felt by the medical officers in charge. The relations between nurses and patients should also be quietly noted. Is a spirit of kindness and gentleness apparent in the place? Are the whims of the aged, the fault-finding of the nervous, the exactions of children, and the apprehensions of the timid met in a proper manner? Is the charitable work of the hospital performed in a charitable way? Do the physicians and nurses display that enthusiasm and *esprit du corps* which are essential to good hospital work?

The subjects which come under the observation of the hospital visitor will vary in different hospitals and at different times; but in general they will include the cleanliness and good order of the wards and the service rooms, the character of the food and mode of serving, the sufficiency of the heating and ventilation, the mode in which the work of the laundry is done, the appearance, dress, and behavior of the nurses and of the other employés, the neatness of grounds and out-buildings, the completeness of the records, and the opinions of patients and their friends as to the manner in which the sick and wounded are cared for in the institution. Scrutiny of the expenditures and approval of bills may also be a part of the duty of hospital visitors.

As regards cleanliness, especial attention should be given to the presence of dust on ledges or projections of all kinds, or on mouldings of doors and windows, on the tops of cases and cupboards, on upper shelves, on the valves of fresh-air registers, etc., as well as on the floor, window-sills, tables, and other places where it is most likely to attract attention. Dust is a dangerous thing in a hospital, and it cannot be removed by sweeping or by what is commonly called "dusting," for these processes merely tend to scatter it, to diffuse it in the air, and to increase its dangers. Rubbing or pressing a surface with the tips of the fingers, or with a white handkerchief, will often show that a surface has not been properly cleaned, when the eye alone might not detect anything out of the way.

The visits should be both regular and irregular. The regular visits should be made on stated days at a certain hour, when it is to be presumed that the hospital will be seen in its best condition. Other occasional visits should be made at irregular and unexpected times, especially at times when meals are being served.

The visitor should sometimes make his inspection alone, sometimes in company with the superintendent, one of the physicians, or the head nurse of a ward, being careful on the one hand not to interfere with the work of the employés, especially in visits at irregular hours; and on the other to avoid all appearance of secret espionage. Do not try to look into everything at one visit.

Visitors should endeavor to see other hospitals besides the one in which they are specially interested. They should read the "Handbook for Hospitals of the New York State Charities Aid Association," Dr. A. Worcester's "Small Hospitals," Miss Isabel A. Hampton's "Nursing," Mrs. M. A. Boland's "Handbook of Invalid Cooking," and Lippincott's series of "Practical Lessons in Nursing."

Taking the several departments of the institution in succession, we will briefly indicate the important points to be observed.

1. **The Ward.**—Is there a perceptible odor on entering it? If so, to what is it due? To iodoform or some other drug; to a recent discharge from the bowels; to the exhalations from a particular patient? or is it merely a vague, slightly musty odor, which

gives a sense of oppression, indicating insufficient ventilation? Is the room too warm or too cold? Note the temperature by the thermometer, which should be present. Are the openings for the entrance of fresh air, and for the exit of foul air, really open, or are some of the registers partially or entirely closed, and, if so, why? What is the general appearance of the ward as to neatness and order? are the beds in line; bedclothes clean and uniform in appearance; the unoccupied beds neatly made? Are there extra beds in the ward? Is it overcrowded? Is the bedside table in proper position? is the top clean and dry? Is there anything on it which ought not to be there,—soiled plates, cups, or spoons, fragments of dressings, etc.? If the patient is in bed, are his clothes in the vicinity? on the chair? on the head of the bed? What is the rule about these things? Are the hands and face of the patient clean? Is his sputa-cup in an unsightly condition?

Does it contain a disinfecting fluid? What are the rules about the use and cleansing of sputa-cups, and are they enforced?

Is the floor smooth and clean? are there any untidy wide cracks or rough places due to knots or tearing off of splinters? Are the floors swept, scrubbed, or cleansed by rubbing with damp cloths to remove the dust? Are the walls and window-sills clean? What is the condition of the medicine-closet as to cleanliness and neatness of arrangement? What is the condition of the bath-room? is there anything in the tub? are dishes or clothes ever rinsed or washed in it? Where are the brushes, brooms, floor-cloths, scrub-buckets, etc., kept, and are they in good condition? Is there a bath thermometer, and is it used when a bath is taken? Is there any rule about turning on the cold water first?

Is there any odor in the lavatory or water-closet? Are there any leaky fittings? What is the condition of the walls, floor, and fixtures as to cleanliness? What is the condition of the urinals?

Is the nurse clean and neat in dress? Does she ever sit on a bed? Does she stand with her hands on her hips? Does she taste the food in the presence of the patient? Does she talk about the patients' cases in their presence? Are her records properly kept? Is she quick to observe what occurs in her ward?

Is there a peremptory rule that hot-water bags or cans are never under any circumstances to be left in the beds of delirious or unconscious patients? Where are the soiled bedding and clothing kept? How often are they taken away to the laundry? What is the condition of the linen-room as to neatness and cleanliness? Is it ventilated? What is the condition of the tea-kitchen? Look in the cupboard and table-drawers, and into the refrigerator, if there is one. If there are projecting ledges, tops of closets, etc., where dust may gather and which are within reach, press the fingers on them and see if they are soiled.

What are the provisions against fire? Buckets filled with water, hose, fire-extinguishers, fire-escapes,—are they in condition for immediate use?

2. The Kitchen and the Serving of Food. —What is the condition of the kitchen utensils as to cleanliness and neatness of arrangement? Where are the dish-towels hung? and are they clean?

Is there a regular diet-list varied for different days of the week? If so, is it adhered to? Are the meals served punctually? What is the quality of the food supplied? What is the condition of the refrigerator or cold store-room? Are milk and butter kept in the same compartment as the meat? Are there any evidences of waste in the kitchen? How is the kitchen refuse disposed of? How are the meals served to patients in bed, or in private rooms? Is the china chipped or cracked? Are the knives, forks, and spoons in good condition? Are the trays neatly arranged? Are napkins used? Is the food well cooked, and hot when it should be hot? Try the coffee, the tea, the bread, the butter, a broiled steak and a chop, the rice pudding.

3. The Laundry.—How is the soiled clothing brought to the laundry? in bundles? in bags? in metal-lined vessels? Are articles from cases of typhoid, diphtheria, erysipelas, or other contagious diseases brought in separate vessels, and how are such articles treated before being put with the general wash? Is a list of the articles to be washed sent with them to the laundry? Are articles stained with blood or excreta soaked in cold water before they are washed in order to prevent permanent staining? Are the articles in satisfactory condition as regards cleanliness and dryness when they are re-

turned from the laundry? Are they free from a laundry odor? Are they listed when they are returned?

4. The Pharmacy.—Note general condition as to neatness and cleanliness. Is a separate account kept of the liquors, wine, and beer ordered for patients? If so, note who orders the most of each kind. The inspection of the pharmacy is, to a great extent, a technical matter not within the scope of the duties of an unprofessional hospital visitor.

5. The Operating-Room, or Amphitheatre. —The fittings and appliances in this room are more or less technical in character, and only the general neatness and cleanliness of the place can, as a rule, be inquired into by the visitor. The instruments should not be packed away in small cases put in dark cupboards; the best way of keeping the great majority of them is on glass shelves in glazed cases. Is there a list of the instruments and apparatus, and is it properly kept up to date?

**6. Store-Rooms, Cellar, Servants' Rooms, Nurses' Rooms.**—The points to be attended to in examining these rooms do not differ materially from those which would receive consideration in a private dwelling,—namely, cleanliness, neat and orderly arrangement, freedom from dampness, light, and ventilation. Note condition of water-, steam-, and soil-pipes as regards leakage; also condition of fresh-air ducts leading to indirect heating coils. Can the cellar air get into these ducts? Note articles stored in cellars and their condition.

**7. Mortuary, or Dead-Room.**—Is this clean and free from odor? Are "specimens" kept in sight? Are the rules with regard to post-mortems properly enforced? What precautions are taken with regard to the bodies of those dying from contagious disease? How are the soiled towels, sheets, etc., sent from the mortuary to the laundry? Have any traces of rats been seen in this room or building?

**8. Grounds, Stable, Carriage-Sheds, etc.—** Are these neatly kept and in good order? Are the ambulance, horse, and harness in good condition? Are there any accumulations of stable manure or refuse, or of ashes? What is the condition of the fence or wall, gates, roads, lawn, trees, back yard, etc.? What disposition is made of ashes and garbage?

**9. Office and General Management.—**Are the relations between the nurses and the resident physicians what they should be? Are they decorous and proper, or characterized by a spirit of levity and undignified familiarity? Is the register of patients properly kept up to date? Are the diagnoses for new patients promptly furnished by the medical staff? Is there an alphabetical index to the hospital register? Is there a record-book of property belonging to patients, and is it properly kept? Are the hospital accounts kept in accordance with the rules? Are the "letters received" properly filed for convenient reference? Are copies kept of "letters sent"? Is a list of donations kept? Is there a library for the use of patients? If so, what is its condition? Are the rules with regard to the admission and discharge of patients, with regard to the admission of visitors, and with regard to leaves of absence for nurses and patients enforced? Is there any case of contagious disease in the hospital? If so, is it properly cared for? Are any of the employés sick? If so, inquire into it a little and see if you can give any assistance. What is the general condition of the hospital as to good order and discipline? What complaints have been brought to your notice which you think of sufficient importance to record, and what are your recommendations, bearing in mind that you should hear both sides?

It is impossible to give a uniform set of forms to be filled out by hospital visitors, since each hospital will require some variation, but we append some simple forms as suggestions which may be modified to suit each case. An ordinary memorandum block of note or letter size, on each page of which the proper headings can be written, is as convenient as anything for making notes. But such notes should always be made in writing, either during or immediately after the visit, and should be made in a certain definite order, such, for example, as that suggested above. Just before making the next inspection the visitor should refresh his memory by the aid of these notes in order to see whether the defects previously observed still persist. At times the visitors may wish to report special defects in the plan or arrangement of the building, in the heating and ventilation, or in the lighting, or may call attention to probable excess or deficiency of attendants or nurses; but detailed suggestions on these points would be out of place in this brief pamphlet.

Finally, let the hospital visitor remember that criticism and fault-finding are by no means his or her sole duty. Note also the good work done, the efficiency with which duties are discharged, the difficulties which have been overcome, the ingenuity and taste which have been displayed. Vague, indiscriminate praise is to be avoided, but intelligent, discriminating commendation of really good points is often a powerful stimulus to further improvement.

## II.—ASYLUMS, HOSPITALS, OR RETREATS FOR THE INSANE.

Many of the above suggestions with regard to the inspection of an hospital apply also to the examination of an asylum for the insane; but in the latter the visitor must give a much greater share of his attention to the condition and mode of management of the different classes of patients. On the one hand he will be appealed to by patients who claim that they are improperly detained, or who have complaints to make about attendants or other patients; and on the other hand there will be a considerable number of patients who can give him no information whatever, and some who will become excited and injured by an attempt at an interview. In many asylums the nurses and attendants are of a different class from the trained female nurses in our best hospitals, and their methods of dealing with patients are not under such constant supervision and inspection as is the work of a hospital nurse. To form a reliable judgment as to the extent to which mechanical restraint is employed, or as to whether there is a sufficient number of proper attendants, is often a difficult matter. Regular periodical visits, the time of which can be foreseen by the asylum employés, are not likely to bring to light certain defects which have been known to exist in many of these institutions, and, therefore, unexpected and

c

frequent visits are more needed to make sure of the true state of affairs than is the case with regard to hospitals. The book of Charles Mercier, "Lunatic Asylums; their Organization and Management," will be found interesting and useful to the asylum visitor.

The following points should receive special attention from the visitor :

1. **The Attendants.**—Have they received special training? Are they good-tempered and forbearing, and also firm and decided? What are their instructions and methods in dealing with a violent patient? Are they neat, tidy, respectful, kind, tactful, quiet, and gentlemanly or lady-like in bearing? Do they have the manner of nurses upon the sick, or of guards in a house of detention? Do they reply to the inquiries and requests of patients kindly and promptly? Are attendants careful to visit the rooms of such persons as are in seclusion regularly and systematically? Are knives, keys, sticks, or

other dangerous weapons allowed in the wards or patients' rooms. Are direct steam radiators covered, so that patients cannot grasp them when heated? Are soiled clothes removed promptly from patients' rooms? Are patients who are wet and soiled promptly attended to? Are clean clothes in every instance put on? Are beds which have been soiled by urine at night washed, or are they simply dried? Are mattresses which are used by untidy patients protected by rubber sheets or mackintoshes, and are such as have become soiled promptly renovated? Is there a plentiful and easily accessible supply of toilet-paper in the water-closets? Is there a night-nurse or attendant constantly on duty in wards occupied by suicidal, timid, untidy, or destructive patients? Are they in sufficient number to insure constant supervision of the patients, so as to give them the greatest possible freedom consistent with the character of their disease? Are patients ever left locked up in wards, or are they turned out into airing courts, without an attendant being present? Are the recent and acute cases, in which there are the greatest possibilities for cure, specially looked after by the physicians and attendants? Do the precautions taken to prevent self-destruction of certain patients unduly limit the freedom and comfort of those who have no suicidal tendencies?

**2. The Food.**—Is it sufficient, well cooked, and of proper variety? Are all patients in the asylum fed substantially alike, or is a difference made in the diet of epileptics, of the maniacal, and of the melancholics? Are the meals properly served, the tables and trays neatly arranged, and the food carefully and economically used? Are the dining-rooms appropriately and sufficiently furnished? In the dining-rooms, are articles of table-furniture used or kept for show? Do patients use knives and forks, tumblers, crockery, etc., at meal-time, or are they furnished with iron spoons, tin cups, and metal plates? Do they have chairs at the table, or are they seated upon board benches which they must step upon in order to get seated? Are the arrangements of the dining-room home-like and comfortable, or do they suggest a poor-house, jail, or pauper institution? Inquire specially as to the quality of the soup, and the amount and variety of vegetables served, and as to whether efforts to reduce expenses are not carried too far in the matter of food. Taste the butter and inspect the bread, milk, and meat.

3. The Clothing of Patients.—Is it sufficiently warm and soft? Does it produce irritation in some patients? Is it adapted to the season? Are the patients' tastes and wishes consulted with regard to their clothing? Is the clothing, especially the underclothing, sufficient in quantity to provide the necessary changes? Is the bedding properly aired before the bed is made? Are the

4

clothing-rooms and the linen-rooms kept constantly in order and well ventilated? Is all the clothing properly and legibly marked? Are articles of woollen clothing and blankets regularly aired and protected from moths? Are articles of clothing in good repair, and provided with buttons? Are pains taken to prevent the clothing of patients of untidy habits from becoming soiled with food? Do patients wear their own clothing, or are they allowed to wear garments belonging to others?

4. **Occupations and Amusements.**—Are patients left to provide these for themselves? Are they used as a mode of treatment? What desires do the patients express with regard to them? Is the supply of newspapers and books sufficient? Are cards, dominoes, draught-boards and men, and chessmen, and materials for other games well supplied? Is there a billiard-table for the use of the patients? Are facilities for

out-of-door games provided? What is the character of the work done for the asylum by patients? How many are employed on each kind of work? How far are the patients allowed to choose their own occupation? Do the assignments to different kinds of work appear to be carefully and judiciously made with reference to the physical and mental condition of individuals? What objections, if any, are made by patients to the work upon which they are engaged? Is the supervision of the work satisfactory? Is tact and good judgment shown in getting patients to employ themselves? Do attendants make drudges of their patients and set them at difficult, disagreeable, or repulsive tasks? Are all the patients who are physically able to go out of doors taken out with regularity for exercise every day?

5. **Precautions against Fire.**—Is there a set of printed or written instructions as to what each employé is to do in case of fire?

Are the attendants familiar with these instructions? Is the apparatus for use in case of fire in good working order? What precautions are taken against fire? Are safety-matches used? Are the floors oiled with linseed oil? What disposition is made of oiled rags? Is a supply of water available in each ward, or are there fire-pails and extinguishers at hand? What standing special directions are provided in the contingency of fire? Is each ward provided with an easy means of escape?

6. **Restraint.**—Are there any patients in restraint or seclusion? If so, are the attendants required to get orders from a physician before resorting to such restraint or seclusion? Is the authority procured before or after the restraint has been resorted to? What means of restraint are used in violent cases? Where are the strait-jackets, muffs, etc., kept? Can the attendant procure them without seeing the physician? Is

the attendant allowed to use his discretion as to their application? What accidents or injuries to patients have occurred in the asylum since the last visit? Investigate each case.

7. **Bathing.**—Are the arrangements for bathing sufficient and satisfactory? Are shower or douche baths used? If so, by whose orders? Is a record kept of their use, and of their effects upon the pulse, temperature, and mental phenomena? Are they properly supervised by the physician? Are patients bathed regularly for purposes of cleanliness, and at what temperature? Is this temperature ascertained by means of a thermometer? Is the bath-tub emptied and cleansed after each patient? Is the patient's head ever put under water as a punishment? Is there an abundance of warm water, soap, and towels?

8. **Care of the Sick.**—Are the discharges of typhoid-fever patients carefully disinfected?

4*

Are there any provisions for cases of diphtheria, scarlet fever, measles, or other contagious diseases? Are the hands and faces of sick patients freshly bathed, the hair neatly brushed, the mouth washed out, the nails cleaned regularly? Is the food for the sick proper in quality and quantity? Are the supplies used carefully and economically, and are all delicacies for the sick put to a proper use?

9. **Night Service.**—Is there a night-watchman constantly on duty at night? Ascertain how his hours are regulated and what check exists upon his movements. Are the sick under constant night nursing? Are epileptic patients kept under observation at night? Are untidy patients visited at regular intervals during the night, and are soiled body clothing and bedding promptly removed and replaced by dry garments and clean bedding? Are suicidal patients carefully watched to prevent accidents? Do

arrangements exist for supplying food and stimulants to the feeble? Can a hot bath be procured at any hour of the night? Is there a regular night service?

10. **Care of the Dying.**—Do nurses sit beside the dying? Are the dead neatly laid out, and are their bodies so disposed of as to be safe from injury or accident prior to removal or interment? In the case of an autopsy, are pains taken to hide all marks of the knife?

11. **Admissions and Discharges.**—Is the law of the State governing the admission and discharge of all classes of patients scrupulously complied with?

# FORMS.

THE following simple forms have been prepared to guide inexperienced hospital visitors in recording the results of their inspections. They will not meet the requirements of all hospitals, and should be modified to suit the peculiar needs of special hospitals. They are intended to be samples of records which may be kept for the private use of the hospital visitor upon successive visits.

44

Date of Inspection.................................189

Hour....................M.

| | WARDS.* | | | | REMARKS. |
|---|---|---|---|---|---|
| | A. | B. | C. | Etc. | |
| General condition of ward. | | | | | |
|     Ventilation. | | | | | |
|     Cleanliness. | | | | | |
|     Beds and bedding. | | | | | |
|     Floors. | | | | | |
| Bath-room. | | | | | |
| Clothing room. | | | | | |
| Dining-room. | | | | | |
| Lavatory. | | | | | |
| Linen-room. | | | | | |
| Small wards. | | | | | |
| Tea-kitchen. | | | | | |
| Water-closets. | | | | | |
| Condition of patients. | | | | | |

G = good; B = bad; C = clean, etc.

* By names, letters, or numbers.

Date of Inspection.........................................................189

Hour...................................M.

| | CONDITION AND REMARKS. |
|---|---|

### Kitchen.

Appearance and dress of cooks.
Cleanliness of broiler.
    "    of carving tables.
    "    of floor.
    "    of food-trays and cases.
    "    of ranges.
    "    of refrigerator.
    "    of tea-, coffee-, and milk-urns.
    "    of utensils of all kinds.
Meat-room.
Milk-room.
Store-room.
Gas and water leaks.
Food-supply.
Quality of cooking.

### Bakery.

Appearance and dress of bakers.
Bread-cupboard.
Bread-pans.
Mixing-tubs.
Moulding-tables.
Ovens.

Date of Inspection...................................................189

Hour...................................M.

| | CONDITION AND REMARKS. |
|---|---|
| **Laundry.** | |
| **Pharmacy.** | |
| **Operating-Room, or Amphitheatre.** | |
| **Store-Rooms, Cellar, Servants' Rooms, Nurses' Rooms.** | |
| Cleanliness. | |
| Neat and orderly arrangement. | |
| Dampness. | |
| Light and ventilation. | |
| Leakage of water-, steam-, and soil-pipes. | |

Date of Inspection.....................................................189

Hour...................................M.

|  | CONDITION AND REMARKS. |
|---|---|
| Mortuary, or Dead-Room. |  |
| Grounds, Stable, Carriage-Sheds. |  |
| Office and General Management. |  |

# BOOKS

SUITABLE FOR

## Nurses and Domestic Use,

PUBLISHED BY

J. B. LIPPINCOTT COMPANY.

# Practical Lessons in Nursing

## I.—The Nursing and Care of the Nervous and the Insane.

By CHAS. K. MILLS, M.D., Professor of Diseases of the Mind and Nervous System in the Philadelphia Polyclinic and College for Graduates in Medicine; Neurologist to the Philadelphia Hospital, etc.

"The book is a valuable one, and should be read by every nurse as well as by physicians who realize the importance of extra-medical influences and agencies in the cure of disease."—*N. Y. Medical Digest.*

## II.—Maternity; Infancy; Childhood.

The Hygiene of Pregnancy; the Nursing and Weaning of Infants; the Care of Children in Health and Disease. Adapted Especially to the Use of Mothers or those Intrusted with the Bringing up of Infants and Children, and Training Schools for Nurses, as an Aid to the Teaching of the Nursing of Women and Children. By JOHN M. KEATING, M.D.

"The first part of the book is intended for mothers,—giving them just that sound, practical advice they so much need, the observance of which must result in healthier women and offspring. For her own sake and for the sake of her child, we wish every mother had a copy of this book."—*Practice, Richmond.*

## III.—Outlines for the Management of Diet;

Or, The Regulation of Food to the Requirements of Health and Treatment of Disease. By E. T. BRUEN, M.D.

"Physicians cannot be cooks, but have a right to expect nurses to know *how* to prepare the proper food as well as druggists should know how to compound medicines. For this reason the little book will serve a valuable purpose and cannot be recommended too highly."—*Cincinnati Lancet-Clinic.*

If not obtainable at your Bookseller's, send direct to the Publishers, who will forward the books, free of postage, promptly on receipt of the price.

### J. B. LIPPINCOTT COMPANY, Publishers,

715 and 717 Market Street, Philadelphia.

# PRACTICAL LESSONS IN NURSING

12mo.  Extra Cloth, $1.00 each.

## IV.—Fever Nursing.

Designed for the Use of Professional and Other Nurses, and especially as a Text-Book for Nurses in Training.  By J. C. WILSON, A.M., M.D., Visiting Physician to the Philadelphia Hospital and to the Hospital of the Jefferson College; Fellow of the College of Physicians, Philadelphia; Member of the American Association of Physicians, etc.

"Such books as constitute this series are invaluable in the training of nurses, and should be added to the reading course for nurses in all our hospitals.  Dr. Wilson's treatise keeps the series up to the high standard of its predecessors."—*Indianapolis Medical Journal.*

## V.—Diseases and Injuries of the Ear:

Their Prevention and Cure.  By CHARLES H. BURNETT, A.M., M.D., Aural Surgeon to the Presbyterian Hospital, and one of the Consulting Aurists to the Pennsylvania Institution for the Deaf and Dumb, Philadelphia; Lecturer on Otology, Women's Medical College of Pennsylvania, etc.

"The instructions contained in these books are applicable to almost any form of disease, excepting surgical cases.  They can be recommended in the strongest terms to nurses and to physicians, and are well written and very handsomely printed."—*Philadelphia Medical and Surgical Reporter.*

## VI.—Hand=Book of Obstetric Nursing.

By FRANCIS W. N. HAULTAIN, M.D., F.R.C.P. Ed., and JAMES H. FERGUSON, M.D., F.R.C.P. Ed., M.R.C.S. Eng.  *Second Edition.*  Revised and Enlarged.  With 33 Wood Engravings.

"This series of Practical Lessons in Nursing should be in the library of every physician, and should be given by him to the nurse as a means of carrying his patient through successfully, and save him many words and valuable time in explaining to the person in charge just what to do and what to avoid.  There are now five of these little works, and the price is within the reach of all."—*St. Louis Medical Brief.*

---

If not obtainable at your Bookseller's, send direct to the Publishers, who will forward the books, free of postage, promptly on receipt of the price.

## J. B. LIPPINCOTT COMPANY, Publishers,

715 and 717 Market Street, Philadelphia.

www.ingramcontent.com/pod-product-compliance
Lightning Source LLC
Chambersburg PA
CBHW021552270326
41931CB00009B/1184